I0423054

Self-Love:

Start Loving Yourself

and Change the World

A Self-Help Guide to Changing

Yourself and Creating a Happy Life

Amber Rich

Table of Contents

Introduction: Where It All Began

The day you were born, in fact, the day you were conceived, your journey began. As you grew and had experiences, some that you enjoyed and others that hurt, you shaped a picture of yourself in your mind that is, right now, influencing the way you see yourself and the rest of the world around you.

This book is intended to give you an opportunity to look at yourself through new eyes, to take down those filters you've created and chosen the path you'll spend the rest of your life on.

On this new path you will know Freedom in a way you probably never fully imagined, and, most of all, you will know Love.

No, I am not referring to romantic love or the love of another person.

The Love I speak of here is the Love of Self that will carry you through every other relationship you will ever have, every job you will be employed in, or business you will own and run.

It will shape every choice you will make from this day forward if you embrace and accept the Truth of the message to you in these pages.

No one is responsible for your life. No one can determine the quality of your life and your experience of it. That is squarely on your shoulders and, as soon as you know this to be true for you in your life, you will see a whole world of possibilities opening up for you.

From the first time you heard the voices of your parents while you were still in the womb, and they felt you moving around, relationships were forming. You were bonding with your mother, and for some of you, the experience was not necessarily a good one.

This first relationship has shaped many relationships you've had since, especially the one you have with yourself. In the gentlest way possible, I hope to show you this and invite you to look at yourself through new eyes, and possibly make some new choices about your relationship with yourself.

No one is going to know you quite the way you know yourself.

It stands to reason then that no one is going to love you quite the way you love yourself, but the way the world and those around you respond to you and treat you will be influenced to a large extent by the way you treat yourself.

This book is about ownership: owning your view of yourself, owning your choices you've made and the consequences that you experience as a result and most of all, owning the freedom you have to make new choices, and to love yourself completely.

I need to be honest with you here. This is a journey that requires Courage. You are going to have to take a long, hard look at yourself, and need brutal honesty to see that you have created the person you are, even the relationships and situations that are uncomfortable for you, takes a huge leap across that ravine of the Unknown parts of you.

Once you can accept that only you can determine the direction and quality of your life and that it starts with your relationship with yourself, you are empowered to change it.

My Story

Once I asked my husband how much he loves me. He was very surprised and asked this question that made me think that his feelings have cooled down. It seemed to me that my husband began to give me less attention and care, I did not have his love, even though everything was as before. Of course, we discussed everything and it seemed that the matter is closed. Some time passed and I began to ask similar questions to my husband more often. I knew that my claim about him was unfounded, his behavior towards me was almost flawless, but something in me caused uncertainty and even suspicion. It is not strange that there was tension in our relationship.

Based on the thesis that everything in the world begins with us, step by step, I have come to understand the shocking truth, you might say enlightenment.

In fact, I did not have self-love. Husband's love, I tried to compensate for this. In other words, I would like to receive love from the outside, not the inside.

Apparently, life's vanity twisted me so that out of my attention fell the most important thing – myself. I accumulated irritability and dissatisfaction with myself, besides the constant criticism of myself and the most dangerous - failure myself. Self-acceptance is the foundation of self-love!

I thank the Universe, for that gave me insight and gave me a chance to change their lives. It is important to realize that we are our mainstay, the core around which revolves our lives. And the more we are harmonious, the happier we are. This understanding did not come immediately. Finding the strength to change yourself is not easy, but it is even more difficult to turn new knowledge into a stable habit. I think you understand what I'm saying.

Therefore, in this book, not only I share my conclusions on the important components of self-love, but also bring practical examples that helped me learn how to love, appreciate and respect myself. Honestly, my life has not turned into an ideal, but it did become much more harmonious and happier. Through loving myself, I was able to understand how to love others, and was able to accept people as they are, without asking anything in return. I took the world with all its beauty and imperfection and the world around me meets the same! And most importantly, I saw new horizons and I had strength to achieve them.

I will be very happy if my experience will help you, my dear reader. Even if you take for yourself a small particle, it would mean that worked on the writing of this book is not in vain.

Thanks for purchasing this book. I hope my book will bring you not only the benefits but also the pleasure.

Chapter 1

Do we understand the self-love correctly?

Self-love is a positive attitude towards oneself, which is expressed in actions. Self-love is manifested through the acceptance, self-understanding, self-esteem, self-kindness and, of course, taking care of oneself.

Of course, taking care of oneself is present every day. We eat, take a shower, go to the doctor, dress for the weather, read books, etc. We do take care. In most cases, it looks like a covering of common needs and sometimes indulging of our whims and weaknesses. But do we love ourselves by doing this?

From the view of self-love, taking care of yourself, your body, mind, spirit and soul must bring inner joy from the process. Only in the case of a genuine desire to take care of yourself will the soul will be filled with warmth and light and the body filled with energy.

Don't confuse self-love with narcissism. The difference between these concepts is huge. Self-love is a deep, holistic, harmonious expression of yourself. Narcissism is a superficial, often with no background, and demonstrates only one feature, imaginary qualities, and insignificant achievements.

Self-love is not an expression of selfishness. Selfishness is a complete disregard of the feelings and interests of others. A person who understood the idea of self-love and learnt how to love himself carefully and prudently will be as natural to love and accept others.

The reality is that those who chose to love themselves more initially tend focus on themselves. And it's not surprising that often, other people see these changes as selfishness. Be careful, do not fall into the trap of selfishness.

Danger of lack of self-love

How, in your opinion, do people who don't love themselves look like? What do they feel? Are they successful? What do you think, is it easy to make a relationship with them?

Numerous studies of these problems confirm that the lack of self-love is the cause of many troubles and failures. These people have a disturbed inner balance. They see the world through the prism of self-pity. Resentment towards themselves and other people is the normal state of people who don't love themselves. The guilt leaves them without their own opinion and often they neglect their interests. The jealousy and shame, supported by the lack of confidence destroy the relationships. The fear and constant anxiety are their constant companions.

Beliefs and negative thinking are the cause not only of the named feeling but also of a corresponding behavior and physiological reaction of the person.

The behavioral model of people who doesn't love themselves in most cases contains passivity and inertia. They love to suffer, showing their insignificance, and they're often in the victim position. People with lack of self-love life with the role of losers.

It's proven by science that the inner state of a person affects the health. Many of those who don't love themselves increase the risk of all kinds of physical and psychological illnesses. Allergies, heart problems, digestive disorders, intestinal disorders, neurosis, phobia: it's a small part of the list of all illnesses that lack of self-love and self-acceptance can be the partial of the cause of.

Agree with me, lack of self-love is a very disgusting thing.

How about you and your self-love? I propose you to make a little test.

Self-love test

Responding to some specially selected questions, you'll understand how much do you love yourself. The questions are divided into areas of life where self-love is important.

Body:

1. Do you always pay attention to the signals of your body about hunger and thirst? (Can you stop when you've eaten enough? Do you drink enough water?)
2. Do you have enough physical activity?
3. Do you take care of your skin (protection against the sun's rays)?
4. Do you understand the psychosomatic body signals (when something hurts, do you try to understand what is your body wanting to tell you?)
5. Do you like your body?

Self-realization:

1. Do you have a favorite business that brings you joy?
2. Do you maintain a balance between work and leisure?

3. Do you know your strengths? Do you develop your talents and skills?
4. Are you proud of your achievements and successes?
5. Does your inner balance depend on your material situation?

Self-esteem:

1. Are your thoughts about yourself positive or are you constantly criticizing yourself?

2. Do you like your appearance?

3. Do you get embarrassed when someone praises you?

4. Are you proud of yourself and your actions or you blame yourself for mistakes?

5. Can you defend your position and say "no" or are you always try to please others?

Relationships:

1. Who is in the first place for you, you or the family?

2. Can you give love to yourself or you demand it from your partner?

3. Are you able to express your needs or you wait till your partner guesses?

4. Does the loneliness confuse you?

5. Is it important for you what others think? Do you depend on the opinion of others?

There are no points or pre-made conclusions to score in this test. This allows you to understand by yourself how much do you love and value yourself and how this affects your relationships, success, realization and, in general, the quality of your life. Are you satisfied with your situation?

I think you need to learn how is self-love interconnected with life.

Chapter 2

Self-love in your life

The previous chapter demonstrated you the importance of a positive attitude towards yourself. I hope that the test helped you to understand how do you feel about yourself and how this affects to your life. In this chapter, we'll review in detail how the idea of self-love should be expressed in our life and what actions are needed to take.

The Impossible Mission

No one is responsible for you, except you. It is not only unfair to expect another person to be responsible for any aspect of your life, it is also impossible.

Why do I say that?

Anyone who holds someone else responsible for any aspect of their life has also given away their power over that aspect of their life.

I'll use an example to illustrate the point.

A young person who has just started working for the first time relies on a parent to wake him up in the morning to be on time for work. One night his mother is sick and takes medication before going to bed. She forgets to set the alarm and they all oversleep the next morning. The young man gets angry with his mother for making him late for work, but he has failed to see that it is his responsibility to get to his job on time, and if he respected himself enough as the adult he now is, he would set his own alarm and get himself up and ready in the morning to be on time for work.

Love carries responsibility. When we say we love someone, we are responsible for our actions towards them and the part we play in their lives.

The same can be said in the context of Self-Love. When we love ourselves, we are responsible for our actions towards ourselves.

The impossible mission is making anyone else responsible for our lives. Anyone we are in a relationship with, whether it is a family relationship, or a friendship, or one we've chosen to be in with a partner, requires us to be responsible for ourselves and the part of that relationship that we represent.

When you fully embrace the relationship you are in with *Yourself* and take full responsibility for your actions, which were your choice, you will never be in a position to blame anyone else.

The only person you will be able to hold accountable for what is going on in your life, is the person looking back at you from the mirror.

"No" is a Complete Sentence

The quality of our relationships is determined by the boundaries we set. There is an expression that says we teach others how to treat us, and that is really the Truth. It can be an uncomfortable Truth because it may be difficult to see how being treated badly by someone is our own fault.

Every healthy relationship, including the one we have with ourselves, requires boundaries. Boundaries are the limits to what we allow. If we don't set these in place, we are open to receiving behavior that may hurt us, or cause negative emotions, or even change the way we see ourselves.

If you feel irritated, or angry, or upset often around a particular person, you need to take a long, hard look at what they are doing that sparks that feeling in you.

If the person is a stranger, perhaps they represent a group of people that behave in a common way.

So, the driver that cuts you off in traffic may represent for you a person who disrespects others.

It is very little you can do to change this behavior in the driver that cuts you off in traffic. At this point, the only thing you can change is how you choose to behave in response to that situation.

Choosing to remain calm and just keeping focussed on your own journey and letting them just drive off without giving them a rude hand signal may free you to feel more at peace with the world around you, although the world around you has very little peace in it.

What is important to see in this simple example is that your inner peace and the choices you make to behave a certain way to stay in that peace adds to the overall peace in the world.

Whatever we are feeling, and doing as a result of those feelings, creates those feelings in the world at large. Feelings are contagious. A person who walks into a room and is visibly angry is going to have an effect on other people. Some will feel fear. Some will also start to feel agitated or angry.

The key here is to realize that if we persistently feel something negative in relation to a specific person or circumstance, we need to examine why we are feeling that and address it at its root cause.

In some instances, we may need to say no to something, or someone. If we are being expected to do anything we are not completely comfortable with, there is a 'No' we have to express somewhere in that expectation.
We may even have agreed to do something and then realized that it does not resonate with us. Then it means we go back to the person we made the agreement with and say we cannot continue to do this thing anymore.

Saying 'No' can be the most difficult thing you have ever done, especially to a partner, or parent, or employer, but done respectfully, and within the context of establishing a healthy boundary so that the relationship can thrive, it will be the most empowering thing you have ever done for yourself, and it will be a clear act of Self-Love that will significantly change the quality of your life.

The Value of Emotions

As mentioned in the previous chapter, we feel emotions in relation to how we are being treated.

Emotions are a really valuable tool on the path of Self-Love. Any emotion, whether positive or negative, says something about you in context with the person or circumstance you are feeling that emotion to.

Emotions are a measurement of the respect and love we need to thrive in our lives.

If we feel strong negative emotions about the way a partner is treating us, and we don't do anything to change it, we will eventually start feeling strong negative emotions about ourselves.

- *Anger*
- *Fear*
- *Distrust*
- *Hate*
- *Disrespect*
- *Pain*

When you read these words, does anything come up for you? Is there one that stands out for you now?

Ask yourself why? Examine under which circumstances you have felt that most recently, or frequently.

Now, consider that the person or circumstance you found yourself with or in is NOT responsible for the way you felt.

Consider the possibility that there is something you need to change to feel differently in the presence of that person, or in that circumstance.

It might not be obvious at first what the change needs to be, but if you can accept that the change sits with you, in either an attitude you have, or boundaries you need to set, or something else, you are already on the path to changing how you feel in that situation.

Whenever I hear someone say, "He makes me so angry", or "She's really pushing my buttons today", I wonder if those people realize that they have given their power away to the person they say is making them feel a particular way.

If they could see how their feelings are self-generated, and that the other person is simply a catalyst to something already going on inside them, they are claiming their power to change the feeling and the results from that place of Self-Love.

Now consider some of these positive emotions:

- *Happy*
- *Contentment*
- *Joy*
- *Comfort*
- *Pleasure*
- *Fun*

Go through the same process as above, and again, realize that the person or circumstance you are feeling these things in relation to are only a catalyst for the expression of something inside you that generates these feelings for you, you are also owning your power to feel these emotions. No one else in your life will ever need to be held responsible again for your happiness, or contentment.

You will be empowered to feel strong, positive emotions purely as a result of your own internal relationship with yourself.

Roles – A Limiting Factor

From our first relationships, within our families, we see and experience role definition. We see a mother, a father, brothers and sisters, and we are the child or sibling in that situation. We go to school and see teachers, and become scholars and students. We start working and become employees. Or we start a business and then we are the employer.

Our lives are filled with roles. We are a member of a soccer team, or a golf club, or a cheer leader squad, or the gymnastics or chess teams.

Our need to belong drives the need to define roles, because once we can identify the role, we will know what is expected of us.

We go on to be someone's wife or husband, and then the cycle starts to repeat itself as we become parents.

There are accepted norms for the behavior of a parent, or teacher, or employer and employee.

The people who challenge those norms are considered rebellious and dysfunctional if they challenge the norms in a way that is perceived to be negative.

Just falling into a role and doing so without a healthy understanding of who we are beyond the scope of that role, and knowing what we believe is best for us and those we are relating to in that situation, may well leave us feeling resentment or guilt, or some other destructive feeling that breaks us down as a person.

In these roles, we may be required to act selflessly, or in other words, always putting others first.

A very common example would be a mother and wife. It is an accepted norm that in this role a woman needs to put her family first. She will be labeled a bad mother, or a selfish spouse if she does anything that puts herself first.

This is obviously a generalization, but I trust it highlights the point that before she became a mother and a spouse, she was a woman, with interests and hobbies, and an intellect, and a Spirit, and a sense of purpose. If she is expected to give up those aspects of herself to be the mother and spouse her family or community expect her to be, she is probably going to feel empty, and unfulfilled in significant areas of her life.

The Purpose of Relationships

So if roles are a limiting factor to our Self-Love, what then is the purpose of relationships? We seem, as humans, to have an inherent need to pair off into a coupled relationship and build a life together with that person. It is a societal norm. It is unusual for someone to choose not to be in a relationship, or have a family.

Relationships are, at the very highest level of purpose, a mechanism through which we get to see aspects of ourselves that need to be healed.

The parts of our spouses or partners that trigger emotions in us, whether we deem them to be negative or positive, are flags waving in the wind to show us where we've buried our treasure – the treasure of our True Selves.

If we experience feelings that we are uncomfortable with in the context of our relationship, it is an indicator that we need to heal something within ourselves, and something needs to change.

It may require having the courage to say 'No' to certain behaviors, of which the most extreme would be abuse. Abuse takes many forms, such as verbal, emotional and physical abuse. It is sad that so many relationships have these abuses in them, and although it is a reality for so many people on a daily basis, I honestly believe it is an aspect of our human journey we are in need of changing.

People in relationships are not isolated from their communities. They, in fact, form the units from which community is built, and the strength of communities is reliant on the strength of the relationship units individual relationships make up.

It is no wonder then that the world seems to be in a sorry state, with constant conflict flaring up in cities and countries all over the world.

To change this is possible, and it filters right down to the people in relationships. Creating healthy relationships creates healthy communities, and this, in turn, creates a healthy world.

Yes, you have the power to change the world!

It starts with the relationship you choose to be in, and the healthy boundaries you set for yourself with your partner.

Self-Love, knowing yourself, knowing what feeds your Soul and Spirit, what inspires you, or hurts you, are all part of the process towards a healthy relationship with your partner.

If you are in a place where you can recognize the relationship you are in to be unhealthy in some way, you have probably identified some form of abuse. If you have taken steps to setting healthy boundaries and these have not shifted the quality of your relationship because your partner is refusing to accept responsibility or make changes to show respect for your boundaries, there may be no other course of action left for you but to leave the relationship.

This may be the most challenging act of Self-Love you have ever had to make, and you may even be called selfish, or self-absorbed, or the reason the relationship didn't work. It doesn't really matter. Until you act on your healthy boundaries and take the step away from the unhealthy relationship, you are going to experience the abuse.

In some instances, your partner may respond positively to the boundaries you have set, and this may take your relationship to a new place, and you may then both experience more joy and happiness in your relationship.

It is a gift you have then given each other, and yourselves, in the process.

This is the place where Self-Love is the most evident because in a relationship you already have a person who is close enough to you to witness who you are and who you are becoming as a person. The relationship is just a mechanism which these changes have become possible for you.

Redefining Success

Success appears on most lists of what people want out of life, and yet, when asked to define what that means for them, they struggle to put it in words. For many of these people, until they've taken a long, hard look at what success means for them, they may be inclined to define it as independently wealthy, or to have a big house with a pool, or to own their own business.

Success is an abstract concept. The cars, and the money and the big house are the results of success as we perceive it, but not necessarily the success itself.

I invite you to take some time on this, write notes on it, whatever comes up for you when you set some time aside to contemplate what Success is for you.

At the risk of prompting you in a particular direction, I would like you to consider that your definition of Success may not be visible in the form of things at all. It may, rather, be identified in a way you want to feel as a constant.

A statement like, "Success for me is freedom to choose the way in which I live my Life." may express a way in which Success will manifest in your Life so that you are able to feel it in the experience of it. Give some thought to this. This is very important as your Self-Love will be expressed through this statement. Every choice you make from that point forward, if it supports the statement, will guide you down a path of Self-Love from one day to the next.

Now is the only time there is

There is no doubt that the pace of life has picked up to the extent that we rush from one place and event to the next, and even sleep and rest periods are sacrificed or put off to get everything ticked off our To-Do Lists daily.

This is completely counter to our need for Self-Love because we are constantly compromising the quality of life we desire to get all these things done.

Taking time for yourself, to exercise, or meditate, or write a journal, or paint, learn to play the guitar, or just walk your dog, are all acts of Self-Love. Deep down we all know that we need to do this, no matter how busy life gets, it is essential to make sure you are strong and balanced in your body, mind, and Spirit.

Let's face it, when you are sick, or exhausted, or too stressed to function normally, you are unable to give your best to your children, your partner or your employer or clients.

You will make poor financial decisions. You will eat too much junk food. You won't drink enough water or get enough sun or fresh air.

It won't be long before you will start questioning what all this is for because you will feel depleted, an empty vessel.

All I can do here is to encourage you to take some time for yourself. Take a walk. Walking is a therapeutic way of processing problems and challenges, and as you walk, the solutions may start to flow. Taking your direct focus off your daily challenges may be just what you need to do for the solutions to present themselves.

The shift in your mindset here is that you realize the value of the moment of Now and that it really is the only time you have to do what matters most for your life.

Constantly putting things off to a future date is saying to yourself that you don't matter, that everyone else and everything else matters more.

If you buy into this lie, you are going to reach a point of resentment or even guilt.

So before you end up in a personal crisis, set time aside for yourself, and know that you are taking care of the most important person in your life – You – and that your family, and boss, and friends, and clients will all benefit from your new energy and creative flow.

Be Gentle with Yourself

We really do beat ourselves up on a daily basis. We bought the wrong milk, or forgot to put out the trash, or locked our keys in the car. Life happens, and it doesn't discriminate. We all have challenges on a daily basis. Lighten up a little. Laugh at yourself. If you don't get through everything on your list today, just reprioritise for tomorrow. Be your own best friend. Stop behaving like an enemy or critic. Ask for help. You don't need to be everyone's superhero. When you are tired, rest.

Watch how water flows. It will take the path of least resistance and yet, is still powerful enough to carve out canyons. There are strength and beauty in that.

Create a Sanctuary

Creating a sanctuary, a quiet place where we get to just be still and centred on ourselves, may seem like a luxury at first, but when you have this space and are using it on a regular basis, you will see the benefits it has for every aspect of your life, and it will become your haven.

Practically, it may not be available to you to have this space set aside permanently in your home. It doesn't have to be bigger than the space surrounding a chair or cushion on a floor, but there are some key requirements for this space to work optimally for you.

- ✓ *It needs to be quiet.*
  If this means your partner takes the children for a walk or plays with them outside for a half an hour every day, then ask him or her to do this for you;
- ✓ *Light a candle.*
  The simple act of lighting a candle is the switch that puts you into 'Me-Time' mode and starts the process of relaxing.
- ✓ *No interruptions.*
  Switch off your mobile phone, the television, the radio, and anything else that may disturb your peace and quiet.

✓ *Feed your senses.*
Play soft, instrumental music or a meditation CD. The sounds of the ocean, or wind through trees, or birds in nature, are all very calming to the Spirit. Also, use an incense stick with your favorite fragrance, or a few drops of an aromatherapy oil on a cotton bud close to you so your personal space is filled with its scent;

✓ *Breathe.*
Breathe slowly, and deeply, down into your diaphragm, and be aware of how your body feels and the thoughts that are moving through your mind. Use your breath to still them.

Know that you are giving yourself a gift in setting this time aside for yourself, and teaching Self-Love in this manner to your children will give them a priceless gift for their own lives.

Date Night

Before you can really know what you enjoy and how you want to be treated by a partner, you need to show yourself some love and respect and dedicate some time to yourself to do activities that you really enjoy. Take yourself on a date once in a while. Even if you are in a relationship with the most wonderful, caring partner, it is unlikely that you will get to do everything you enjoy with them all the time.

Taking time alone to go to a movie only you would enjoy, and eating in a restaurant you enjoy more than your partner does, or just doing things alone that others in your life don't enjoy, is a way to exercise Self-Love and keep that which is sacred to you, alive.

If you are not in a relationship at the moment, taking yourself on a date is probably even more important for you, rather than sitting at home wishing someone else would. When you are giving yourself what you feel you need, you don't need anyone else. Your motivation for going on dates with others will then be driven by a genuine desire to get to know them, rather than filling a void in your life.

People want to feel seen and heard in a relationship. You are doing yourself and your current or future partner a great service by always being willing to take care of your own needs. This way you cannot form unhealthy dependencies on others and you won't be wasting valuable time in your life feeling lonely when you could have been enjoying yourself instead.

There are many options in terms of 'Date Night'. If you are not a fan of dining out or going to movies on your own, start a book club, or movie and dinner club, and make it available to other single people you know. Hobbies are a great way to gather with other like-minded people. Learn to sew, or fly model airplanes, or sign up for a language course at a local college.

While you are doing all these things you will feel the satisfaction of having developed new skills or talents, and you will have widened your friendship circle in the process.

Be the Centre of Your Universe

You are going to love many people in your life. Not all of them are going to be with you for your whole life. Even those who promise to be with you always may not be able to do so, as a result of illness or death.

There is only one person that will always be a constant in your life, and that is YOU.

When you take a flight on an airplane the flight attendant will explain to you at the beginning of the flight all the procedures to follow in the event of an emergency. One of these instructions is that if you are a parent, you need to place your own oxygen mask over your own face FIRST, and then assist your child with theirs. You are no good to them if you are unconscious, so right there, on your next flight, you will hear why Self-Love is important – it not only preserves your life but also ensures that you are then fit and able to assist those around you.

Chapter 3

What should you do to love yourself?

In order to love yourself, you'll have to work hard on yourself. You have to completely review your life scenario, change the conscience and learn how to interact with the world from the position of "I am a valuable, respect and love-deserving person". I'm sure that you realized it when reading the first half of the book.

The old beliefs, negative attitudes, stereotypes, low self-esteem and, of course, the internal resistance will be trying to disturb you. That's why I need you to be aware and perseverant and the methods and tools proposed in this chapter will help.

What do you need to do:

1. Change the negative attitudes about yourself;
2. Raise your self-esteem;
3. Learn how to quickly relieve stress and relax;
4. Properly structure your life from the position of a successful and productive person. You can read about it in my book «*Manage Your Productivity: A Stress-Free Personal System*

to Improve Your Productivity, Create Effective Habits and Beat Procrastination».

Next, we'll review the methods and exercises that will help you to love yourself.

Love creates self-respect, self-acceptance and the realization of oneself as a unique person with unique advantages and disadvantages. And the lack of self-love creates excessive self-criticism, frustration, indecision, pessimism, the desire to please others and the sense of guilt. With no self-love, it's impossible to have an adequate self-esteem.

Your task is to learn how to evaluate yourself. Don't underestimate or overestimate them. Perform the exercises. The first one will let you understand what qualities you have, the second one will show you what one or other qualities give us.

Exercise 1

Take a clean sheet and a pen. Divide the sheet vertically into 3 columns. In the first column, you write at least 10 names of film, cartoons or book characters or real famous people. The important part is: you have to like them. In the second column (next to each name) write 2-3 qualities that you admire in this character. Calculate how many qualities you got in the end. For example, "justice" – 5 mentions, "patience" was repeated 3 times, "courage", 4 times. Write them down in the third column, in descending order: justice, courage, patience.

Re-read this list. These are your qualities. You chose the qualities that resonate with you, with your soul.

Exercise 2

Take two sheets of paper. Divide them in half vertically. In the first half of the first sheet write a list of qualities or properties of the character that you don't like and you want to get rid of them. By the same principle, in the second sheet write a list of qualities or strengths that you'd like to get. Then, next to each undesired quality describe the situation where this quality could be beneficial. And in relation to each quality from the second list, a situation where this quality would be harmful.

This exercise reinforces the fact that everything in the world is dual. Good and bad things go together and complement each other. Look at yourself with another perspective. Try to evaluate yourself adequately.

The causes of an inadequate self-esteem, as well as of the lack of self-love have their start in childhood. With all our wishes, we cannot change the past. But all we have left is to change our attitude towards those events and create a new script of our life, with a positive attitude and beliefs.

Delete the negative attitudes

Attitudes are unconscious programs that determine our behavior and attitude towards ourselves and the world around us. There are positive attitudes that help us and the negative ones that interfere and limit our possibilities. The negative attitudes can relate to any area of life and, of course, they affect to the self-image, self-love, and self-acceptance.

List of negative attitudes:

1. I don't deserve it.
2. I won't achieve it.
3. I'm worse than my friend.
4. Life is not fair to me.
5. I was born in a wrong time.
6. I have to tolerate, there are people who live worse.
7. I'm angry and offended at my parents that they didn't teach me a lot of things and they didn't love me.
8. I always have to be busy and resting is bad because it means that I'm doing nothing.
9. I invest all my time for a better life in the future.
10. I failed in my life. I'm already 45 and it's too late to start from scratch.

11. There's no certainty in life. I don't know what awaits me tomorrow.
12. I want too much, but everything still remains a dream.
13. I criticize too much myself, I feel dissatisfaction.

This is a very small list of all limiting attitudes. Your job is to detect them as much as you can. It's not easy because negative attitudes are strongly wired into our thinking and are often accepted by our brain as correct.

How to identify negative attitudes?

Be self-observant, analyze the area of life (health, money, relationships, etc.) where you have difficulties, track your thoughts and reactions to the events that are happening. Observe family and friends, you might have similar negative attitudes. Write down all the attitudes on paper. If you approach this process responsibly, the amount of the written attitudes will impress you.

How to eliminate the negative attitudes?

The first step is to realize that you have a negative attitude. Not just a statement of the fact, but a conscious understanding that this attitude bothers you and you must get rid of it.

Next, you should understand the cause of the attitude and **with the help of visualization** you must destroy its corrosive impact. For example, when you have not coped with a management position, even though they had high hopes for you. Now you're afraid of responsibility, you reject the promotion, limiting your development with it. Remember this traumatic situation and your feelings about it in detail. Mentally send those memories to the fire. Imagine how the fire burns them gradually, without even leaving ashes.

Visualization methods can be used as a supportive psychological method to deal with any difficulties (visualization doesn't mean you mustn't act!). Another example of visualization: imagine that you have a barrier in front of you that doesn't let you move forward. The barrier is your negative attitude or difficulty. Imagine, how you easily and happily destroy it with a big hammer. Your problem crumbles into fine dust and the wind carries it away from you...

I really like this method. It's very uplifting.

If you find it difficult to imagine the images, don't worry, you just have another way of thinking. Try using the method of **free writing**. Usually, this technique is used to solve business tasks, generate ideas, and write books or articles.

This method is also very suitable for our purposes. You have to describe in detail the situation, thoughts, and feelings that make you worried and then destroy it (burn it or break into small pieces and throw it out). A tip for you: write all the thoughts in a row without reading what you're writing, without caring about the grammar or style. The time of this exercise has to be short (5-10 min). This approach allows you to study your subconscious effectively. The main goal is to throw out the negative emotions and feelings, detect and delete the unconscious blocks.

Another method of dealing with negative attitudes is to **change the tonality of the attitude**, reprogram its meaning from negative to positive (from "minus" to "plus"). For example, the attitude "If I follow my desires, my family and friends will be offended. I don't want to argue with them." can be changed to "My desires bring me the joy that I share with my loved ones. We are happy." Write down the new behavior; it's your new program that you need to install in your conscious mind. To make sure everything went well you have to check if the statement is true. Your brain needs proofs. Look for them in the outside world. Think about who among the people you know doesn't reject his desires and at the same time everything in his family goes well. Take a closer look and you'll see a lot of similar examples. Negative attitudes were making you see only the confirmations that correspond to them.

The fight against negative attitudes is additionally aggravated by our resistance. We often don't want to get rid of them because it's kind of a psychological defense mechanism. The negative attitudes give us an excuse for the failures. For example, the belief of that nothing depends on you helps you to justify your mistakes and failures.

Negative attitudes help us to put pressure on the pity, so others can feel sorry for us and try to solve our problems. They don't justify our inaction. Why would you do something if you know you'll fail? I'm not smart, I don't have friends, I don't know how to do it. You better feel sorry for me, strengthening my confidence that I won't achieve anything.

The fear of change often stands behind negative attitudes. We are afraid of going beyond the habitual way of life, we're afraid of uncertainty, we're afraid of other people's opinion. But in order to change the life, it is just necessary to get out of the comfort zone. Expand your comfort zone gradually, in a comfortable velocity. For example, take a walk in new places, find a new hobby, change the hairstyle. There are a lot of variants. Just experiment!

There are two similar techniques which help to neutralize the negative attitudes: *affirmations* and *auto training*.

Affirmations

An affirmation is a positively formulated statement-phrase. With frequent conscious repetition of an affirmation, you fix a desirable image or setting into your brain. Affirmations contribute to the improvement of psycho-emotional background and stimulate positive changes.

Examples of affirmations:

1. *I'm a confident person.*
2. *The world is good. I'm safe.*
3. *I love my body and I take care of my health.*
4. *Others respect and love me.*
5. *I like to give joy to others.*
6. *I trust the Universe.*
7. *I know how to make money.*
8. *I'm a magnet for success and good luck.*

How to correctly make and use affirmations:

1. Affirmations should be pronounced in the present tense and not in the future. Correct: "I

deserve love and respect", "My sight gets better every day".

2. The statement should reflect what you want to achieve and not what you're trying to get rid of. Don't use the denial in affirmations and avoid negative moments. For example: "I'm stopping worrying. I don't worry" is not correct. Our subconscious mind doesn't perceive the particle "no", so this way you strengthen your worry. The correct version is: "I'm calm and balanced".

3. Use the action verbs. Our subconscious mind understands them as orders: "I achieve the goals easily and with joy".

4. The affirmation should be easy and understandable, with a meaning. For example: "The success and a good luck are my constant companions".

5. The affirmations are directed to the person who practices them. Therefore, it's right to use "I", "Me", "My". For example: "I'm a valuable employee and I successfully develop my career". "My boss offers me the promotion" isn't correct. You can't affect to another person with your affirmations.

6. Repeat the affirmations regularly a few minutes a day. Approach the process

consciously, with enthusiasm and belief in what you are saying.

The effect of affirmations weakens if the phrase enters in conflict with your body and the expression on your face. Make a little experiment: lower your arms helplessly, make the suffering face and lamentably say: "The world is beautiful! Everything's perfect!" What is the effect? Do you believe in that everything's beautiful? And how's your mood?

And now open your shoulders, straighten your back, lift the chin and say with a cheerful tone: "Everything's bad!" I believe that your mood has improved!

This exercise demonstrates that if you usually live with a negative body posture, even the best affirmations will lose their power. What to do? Monitor your body, accustom yourself to a correct posture, remove the tensions, work with gestures, facial expressions, and intonations.

You can use auto training to greatly facilitate the work with the negative attitudes and to enhance the effect of the affirmations.

Auto-training (AT)

Auto-training is a technique of self-suggestion on the background of a complete removal of muscular and nervous tension. This method was developed by a German doctor, Dr. Schultz J. H in 1932. It's actively used in medicine, sports, pedagogy and in self-education. It helps reduce emotional and physical tensions, restores energy and performance, normalizes sleep, and develops the memory and imagination.

The method is easy enough to understand and use, it's effective and (more importantly) pleasant. Besides, it's a great way to relieve stress and restore the energy before an important event. The auto training teaches how to relax. The relaxed state reduces the critical thinking, balances the emotional state and the person's conscious greatly perceives new positive attitudes.

The auto training technique consists of 3 stages:

1. Stress relief and relaxation.
2. Pronunciation of special verbal suggestions or just relaxation (10

minutes sleep greatly restores the energy with the auto training help).

3. Exit from the relaxation state, return to normal life in the state of vitality and inner harmony.

To make sure the practice went well and brought you the maximum benefit follow these simple rules.

1) Practice auto training when nobody can disturb you. To make it more comfortable you can lie down and close your eyes. Completely relax. Breathe smoothly and quietly.

If your body cannot relax by itself, help it by slowly saying in your mind: *"I'm absolutely calm. My breathing is smooth and quiet. My toes, shins, knees and hips are relaxed. My legs are getting heavy. There's a pleasant warmth going through my legs. My arms are relaxed and heavy. There's a pleasant warmth going through them that slowly goes to the body. My body is also completely relaxed. The heat goes from my solar plexus through the whole body. My head is relaxed. All the facial muscles are relaxed. My breathing is smooth and quiet. I can breathe easily and freely. My body is full of a pleasant heaviness and warmth. My whole body is completely relaxed"*.

If you were able to feel a pleasant heaviness and warmth, that means that you got to relax. Over time, you'll learn how to relax even in the transport. The ability to relax is a very useful skill. Even if the auto training technique is not for you, be sure to practice the relaxation sessions.

2) Choose the words depending on the purpose for which you practice the auto training. You have to formulate the words in positive tones, avoiding the particle "no". For example, say "be braver", instead of "don't be afraid". Get rid of the words like "I'll try" because they mean uncertainty. If possible, stop saying "Now I realize..." It's preferable that you remember the words of the attitude so that you don't get distracted by inventing or remembering them when practicing. Alternately, make an audio recording of your attitude and look on the internet the most suitable for you.

Let's look at an example. Suppose you found difficulties to accept yourself. Undoubtedly, this negative attitude complicates your life a lot. You are full of desire and determination to get rid of it. An example text for the auto training:

"I am me. I am unique and the only one. That's why all that comes from me is truly mine. I own all that is in me:

- *My body, with all its imperfections and natural processes;*
- *My mind, including all my thoughts and plans, hopes and fears;*
- *My feelings and emotions, despite their tone;*
- *My words and actions, the right and the wrong ones.*

I own all my actions, successes, and failures. All that is to me is mine, good or bad. I accept everything with love and gratitude. I get on well with every part of me and this allows me to know who am I and where am I at the moment. I believe that I can improve every part of my character. I belong to myself and that's why I build myself.

Now I realize that I am me and being me is great."

It's not necessary to use big texts for the training in the beginning. For now, you can make a few lines or just choose a few of the most important words. If you practice the auto training regularly, you'll notice in a few months that your brain invents detailed sentences alone.

It's possible that in the process of working with yourself you'll encounter internal resistance. In this case, I recommend you to gradually teach your subconscious that it needs to love itself.

There's a list of affirmations below that will help you. Start with the affirmation "*I want to love and approve myself*". Work with it, until the resistance is gone, and then go to the next phrase "*I can love and approve myself*", etc.

> *I want to love and approve myself*
> *I can love and approve myself*
> *I allow myself to love and approve myself*
> *I know how to love and approve myself*
> *I do everything to love and approve myself*
> *With every minute, I love and approve myself more and more*
> *I love and approve myself*

Over time, the final phrase "*I love and approve myself*" will become a final fact that won't be able to be doubted, and not just an affirmation.

Affirmations and auto training are excellent additional practices that undoubtedly help in expanding and changing the conscience. But let's be honest, they do not change the real state of things. The real changes come after your real acts.

You already have all the knowledge you need and I hope that you realized that the self-love is the axis around which you have to build your new happy life. You risk staying at the same level of happiness and satisfaction that you are now if you don't begin to put into practice the knowledge that you have.

Getting more knowledge just for the sake of quantity is not only unreasonable from the point of view of resources (time, strength, finances), but it's also dangerous. Yes, I mean dangerous. We can get into the illusion that it's enough to just read a book (or multiple books) and everything will change, but the reality brings disappointment and then the hope disappears.

That's why if you really want to be happy and share the happiness with others, start acting and using the knowledge. Act: love, value and respect yourself as fast as possible.

And to make it easier, I've collected a list of 50 methods that will help you. Chose those ones that your soul resonates with. Even if you'll end up using a few very simple methods, this will change your life and well, only if you start to act!

50 methods of how to learn to love yourself

1. Start the day with pleasant words. Recharge yourself with positivity and good mood. Affirmations can successfully help with it.
2. Be kind to yourself, support and motivate yourself.
3. Remember: you are the closest person to yourself. That's why to talk to yourself gentler. Don't criticize yourself too much and do not call out yourself.
4. Keep yourself in good shape. Do physical exercises every day. Your beautiful body deserves your love and care.
5. Eat healthy food, drink more water and sleep 7-8 hours.
6. Talk to people that inspire you. Be ready to end the relationship with those who offend you or treat you badly.
7. Aspire to build relationships with people based on love and respect. Be ready that not everyone will respond to you in the same way.
8. Get rid of toxic personal relationships. Remember that you deserve to be happy.
9. Stop comparing yourself to others. You're a unique person and that's why comparing yourself to other people makes no sense. They're not

better or worse, they're just different. Compare yourself only to who you want to be in the future.

10. Don't look for other people's approval. You don't need it in order to be yourself. It's your life, don't let others live it for you.

11. Accept the fact that some people don't like you. In the end, you won't be liked by everyone. There's nothing bad in this. Don't spend your time on being liked by someone. Be natural.

12. Accept that you are different from others and love this because that is why you are unique.

13. Write love letters to yourself. They will help you to realize that you deserve love.

14. Know your strengths. Appreciate your skills, use and improve them.

15. Praise yourself! You'll already hear the criticism from other people.

16. Let your soul lead you to your dream. Do things that you were constantly postponing.

17. Develop your creativity. The expression (singing, dancing, painting, etc.) will only confirm your uniqueness.

18. Be open to new things. New possibilities will open up for you, so don't refuse them.

19. Get to know yourself. Make effort to know who are you, which true desires you have and what your soul is striving for.

20. Rewrite the inner scenario. Work with the negative beliefs about yourself.

21. Stop scaring yourself. Don't assume the worst will happen, especially when you go to bed. Get rid of generalizations, black and white thinking, and extreme exaggerations.
22. Control your thoughts; suppress the negative ones and focus on the positive thinking.
23. Consciously look at your thoughts and feelings. Learn how to recognize and understand them in terms of usefulness to you.
24. Don't be ashamed to show your emotions and feelings. You are a live person, not a robot.
25. Stop criticizing yourself. Self-dissatisfaction is just a habit.
26. Be proud of yourself. Celebrate all your achievements, both big and small ones.
27. Give gifts to yourself without a reason. You look good when you're happy.
28. Try to stay calm, inner balanced and optimistic in any situation. The panic and despondency are bad friends.
29. Rest. Let your body and mind disconnect for a while. A person who had a rest can do a lot more.
30. Don't regret when you spend time on yourself. Don't feel guilty about it. It's your life, that means it's your time.
31. Remind yourself of the results of self-love. Remember that you'll win in all areas of your life from it. You'll have more energy, which will allow you to have even more control of your life.

32.   Master the techniques of stress relief and relaxation. Practice them every day.

33.   Be patient and stay persistent. Don't expect instant results. Self-love is a continuous process. Aspire to be better today than you were yesterday.

34.   Be grateful for every day that you live, for every success and difficulty. This makes you stronger, smarter and more experienced. Remember at least three things that you're grateful for every morning.

35.   Don't hesitate to ask for help. This is not a sign of weakness. Your family, friends, and colleagues are happy to support you during the trouble.

36.   Start saying "no". Respect your interests and yourself. Surprisingly, others will start to respect you too.

37.   Know how to stand up for yourself. As well as the ability to say "no", this method shows that your opinion and needs are important to you.

38.   Learn how to forgive yourself. You cannot change the past, but you have the control of your future. See the past as experience that will help you to be better.

39.   Don't think about the wounds and offenses from the past. This keeps you in the past and it doesn't allow you to move forward.

40.   Learn how to hear and listen to yourself. Maintain a dialogue with yourself. It'll significantly make your life easier.

41. Be honest with yourself. It's not easy. Sometimes we lie to ourselves like a pro and we don't even realize it.

42. Take off the pink glasses. Live in the reality. Take life as what it is in all its diversity. Don't wait for the ideal life, it doesn't exist.

43. Avoid the perfectionism. Focus on the process and not in the result. Striving for perfection is a load that's too heavy.

44. Learn how to ignore the negativity of other people. You can't influence the other person, you can only influence yourself. Ignore the negativity, let it go.

45. Don't waste your energy on trifles. Our life is full of distractions, it's important to know how to separate important things from useless stuff.

46. Find your place, where you feel good. Go there every time that you need.

47. When you feel happy, make a list of your achievements and best qualities. Re-read it when you have bad moments. This will help you to restore your belief in yourself.

48. Live here and now. Live consciously every moment. Remember: the past already has passed and the future has not yet arrived.

49. Have fun and enjoy. This helps to cope with difficulties. Life is beautiful!

50. Love yourself right now without any conditionality.

Self-Love: Your Gift to the World

We have all come into this world to be a contributing part of it. Every one of us is a Gift to the World in our own way. We all have something unique to offer. Treating ourselves with Love and Respect will result in far less conflict, within us and in our relationships, and it will mean making far fewer decisions that we regret or have to suffer negative consequences from.

In the final analysis, the World can only be a happy, peaceful place when the people living in it are happy and at peace with themselves and each other.

It is impossible for the World to be at war, or in a state of turmoil when the individuals populating the World are all in a state of Self-Love. We cannot harm anyone else, or ourselves when we are caring for and loving ourselves.

Keep Moving Forward

Every day is a new day. Every moment is another opportunity to make better choices and to find new ways of exercising Love and Self-Love. As you make choices with the intended outcomes you expect, accept that things will not always turn out the way you intended. Embrace the opportunity than to learn and make fresh choices with different intended outcomes. As you do this you are making the statement that you know and accept that you are willing to be wrong, and own the consequences, and be open to the possibilities in every circumstance.

In this way you will experience a flow of your life that is gentler and easier to deal with, and you will know in the very deepest part of you that you are creating your life, that you are powerful, and that every good and wonderful thing that you could choose for yourself is possible, because you love yourself, and you always give the best to those you love.

Conclusion

The purpose of this book to show you the importance and value of self-love, to give you the tools you can use to make their lives happier. Love yourself - this is not an aim, it is not selfish, not to show disrespect for others. Love yourself – this is accepted yourself, it is respect, it is to take care of yourself - all this is natural as breathing. For various reasons, we reject the love yourself, thus depriving yourself of happiness and harmony. Allow yourself to breathe, become happy today, do not wait for tomorrow. This book provides you with the help of an algorithm which can learn to love yourself.

What need to do:

- Recognize and accept the principle of the responsibility for your life. This is the basis, the foundation of its kind that allows you to look at life through different eyes, and most importantly will provide an opportunity to take steps towards improvement.
- Learn how to build your personal boundaries, do not be afraid to say "No."
- Allow yourself to feel. Any feelings and emotions - positive or negative - they are yours and they are important in the first place to

you, keep track of them, learn to understand their nature, do not be afraid to show them.

- Review your social roles and if they do not correspond to the concept of a healthy relationship - safely improve.
- Take care of body and soul - this is important in equal measure. Dedicate time exclusively for yourself.
- Appreciate every moment of your life. Live here and now.
- Share your love and energy with others. Be open to other people, the world, and the Universe.
- Do not stop, keep moving forward.

Here are the main components that I use in my life. These are proven rules which I fully trust. I try to bring up my kids according to them. Of course, you can add something of your own, that is important for you and that will help you. Take a step towards yourself, and though it will not be easy and will not immediately, it will bring your happy life. Just start to love yourself now, at this moment, and I'm sure the results will certainly delight. Love and be happy.

Copyright 2016 by Amber Rich - All rights reserved.

All rights Reserved. No part of this publication or the information in it may be quoted from or reproduced in any form by means such as printing, scanning, photocopying or otherwise without prior written permission of the copyright holder.

Disclaimer and Terms of Use: Effort has been made to ensure that the information in this book is accurate and complete, however, the author and the publisher do not warrant the accuracy of the information, text and graphics contained within the book due to the rapidly changing nature of science, research, known and unknown facts and internet. The Author and the publisher do not hold any responsibility for errors, omissions or contrary interpretation of the subject matter herein. This book is presented solely for motivational and informational purposes only.

www.ingramcontent.com/pod-product-compliance
Lightning Source LLC
Chambersburg PA
CBHW060220290526
45789CB00003B/1345